BigTime® Piano

Popular

2010 EDITION

Level 4

Intermediate

Arranged by

Nancy and Randall Faber

Production Coordinator: Jon Ophoff
Design and Illustration: Terpstra Design, San Francisco
Engraving: Dovetree Productions, Inc.

FABER
PIANO ADVENTURES®
3042 Creek Drive
Ann Arbor, Michigan 48108

A NOTE TO TEACHERS

BigTime® Piano Popular is a collection of popular favorites arranged for the intermediate pianist. The selections have been carefully chosen for their broad appeal and arranged to give the student a "big" sound, while remaining accessible at the intermediate level.

BigTime® Piano Popular is part of the *BigTime® Piano* series arranged by Faber and Faber. As the name implies, this level marks a point of significant achievement for the piano student.

Following are the levels of the supplementary library, which lead from *PreTime®* to *BigTime®*.

PreTime® Piano	(Primer Level)
PlayTime® Piano	(Level 1)
ShowTime® Piano	(Level 2A)
ChordTime® Piano	(Level 2B)
FunTime® Piano	(Level 3A–3B)
BigTime® Piano	(Level 4)

Each level offers books in a variety of styles, making it possible for the teacher to offer stimulating material for every student. For a complimentary detailed listing, e-mail faber@pianoadventures.com or write us at the address below.

Visit **www.PianoAdventures.com**.

Helpful Hints:

1. As rhythm is of prime importance, encourage the student to feel the rhythm in his or her body when playing popular music. This can be accomplished with the tapping of the toe or heel, and with clapping exercises.

2. Hands-alone practice is often helpful. Ensure the playing is rhythmic even when practicing hands separately.

3. The songs can be assigned in any order. Selection is usually best made by the student, according to interest and enthusiasm.

4. Chord symbols are given above the treble staff. Time taken to help the student see how chords are used in the arrangement is time well spent. Such work can help memory, sightreading, and the development of improvisation, composition, and arranging skills.

ISBN 978-1-61677-009-9

TABLE OF CONTENTS

100 Years

Words and Music by
JOHN ONDRASIK

6

from *The Phantom of the Opera*

The Music of the Night

Music by ANDREW LLOYD WEBBER
Lyrics by CHARLES HART
Additional Lyrics by RICHARD STILGOE

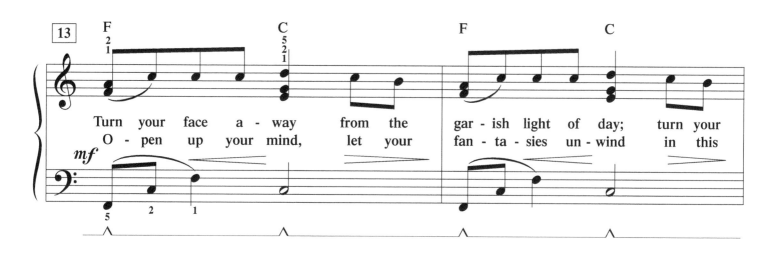

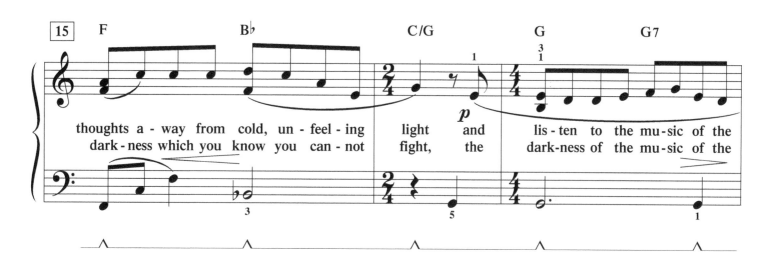

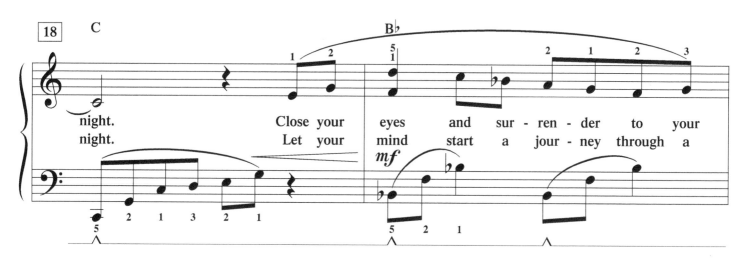

from the movies
Star Wars and *The Empire Strikes Back*

Star Wars (Main Theme)

JOHN WILLIAMS

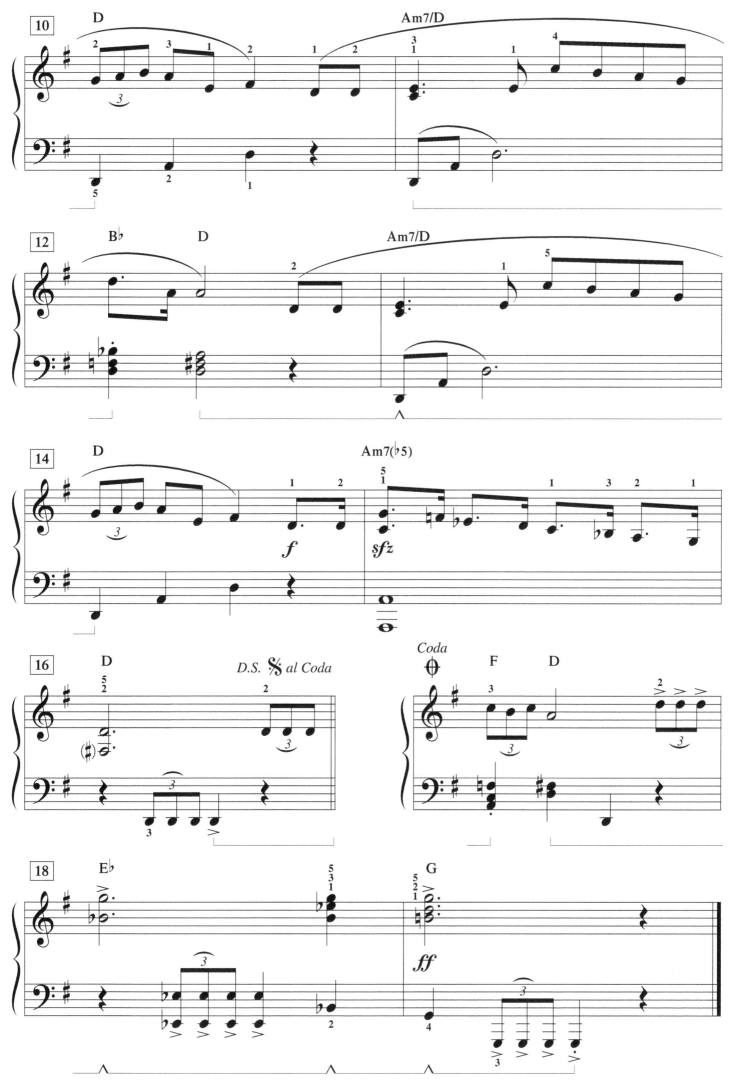

from *Willy Wonka and the Chocolate Factory*

Pure Imagination

Words and Music by
LESLIE BRICUSSE and
ANTHONY NEWLEY

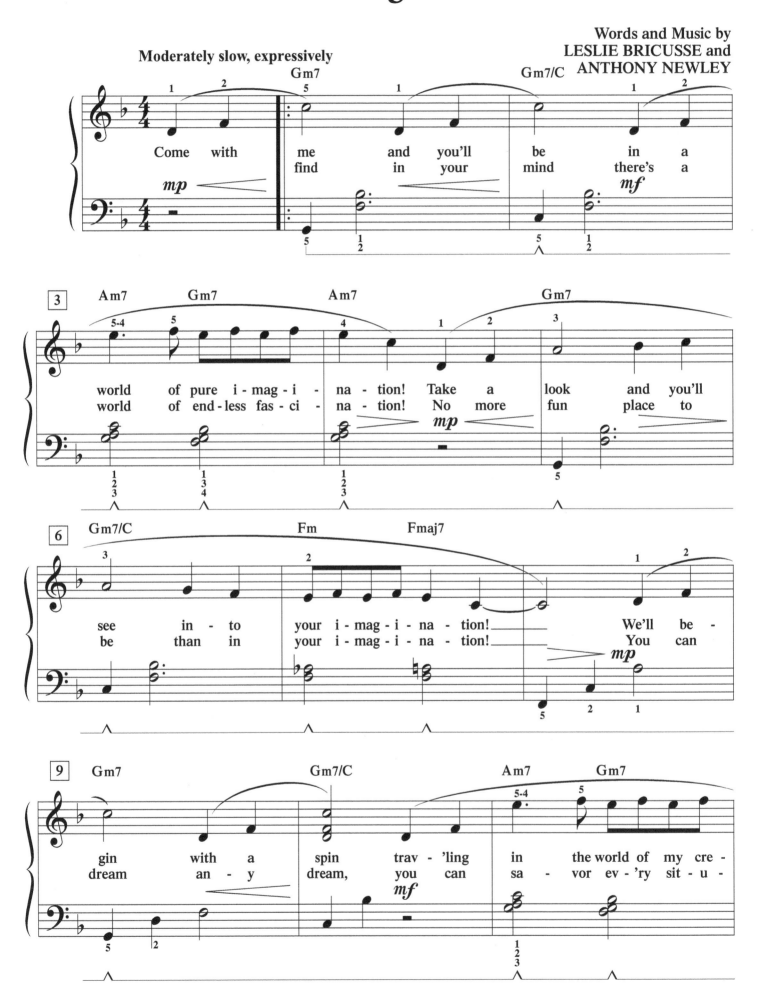

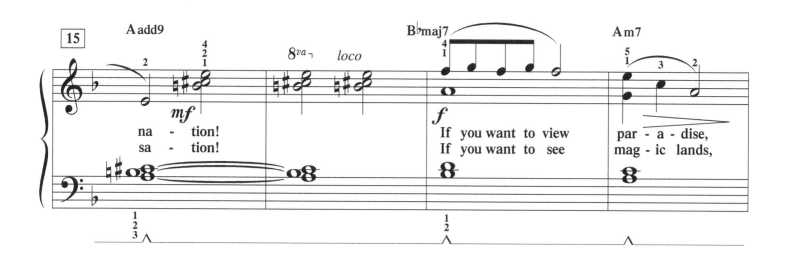

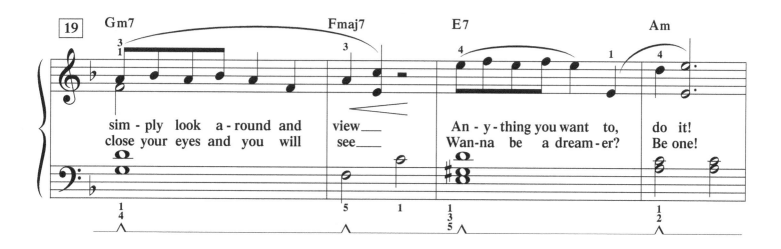

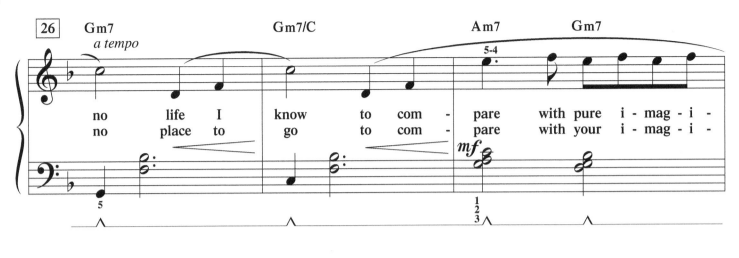

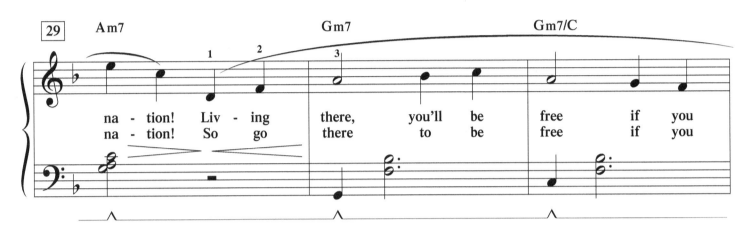

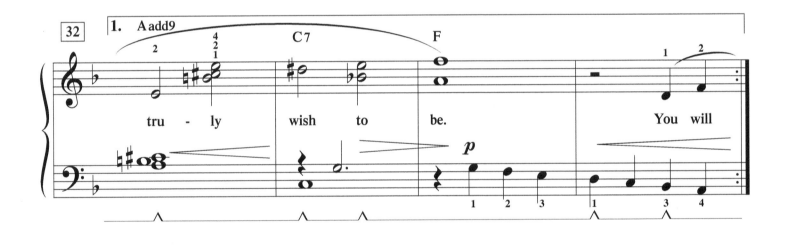

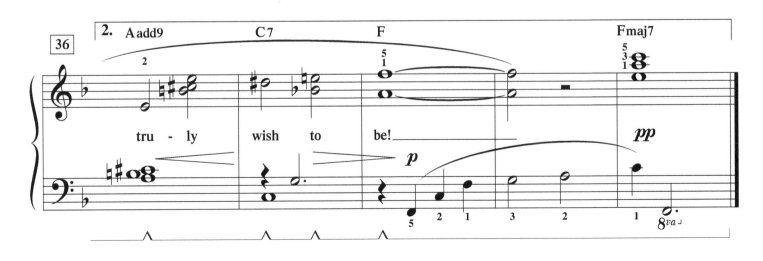

Lean On Me

Words and Music by
BILL WITHERS

FF1009

car - ry on;___ for it won't be long___ till I'm gon - na need___

___ some - bod - y to lean___ on.___ lean___ on.___ Just

call on me, broth - er, when you need a hand. We all

need some - bod - y to lean___ on. I just

might have a prob - lem that you'd un - der - stand. We all

from *Mamma Mia!*
Dancing Queen

Words and Music by
BENNY ANDERSSON, BJÖRN ULVAEUS
and STIG ANDERSON

23

FF1009

You Raise Me Up

Words and Music by
BRENDAN GRAHAM
and ROLF LOVLAND

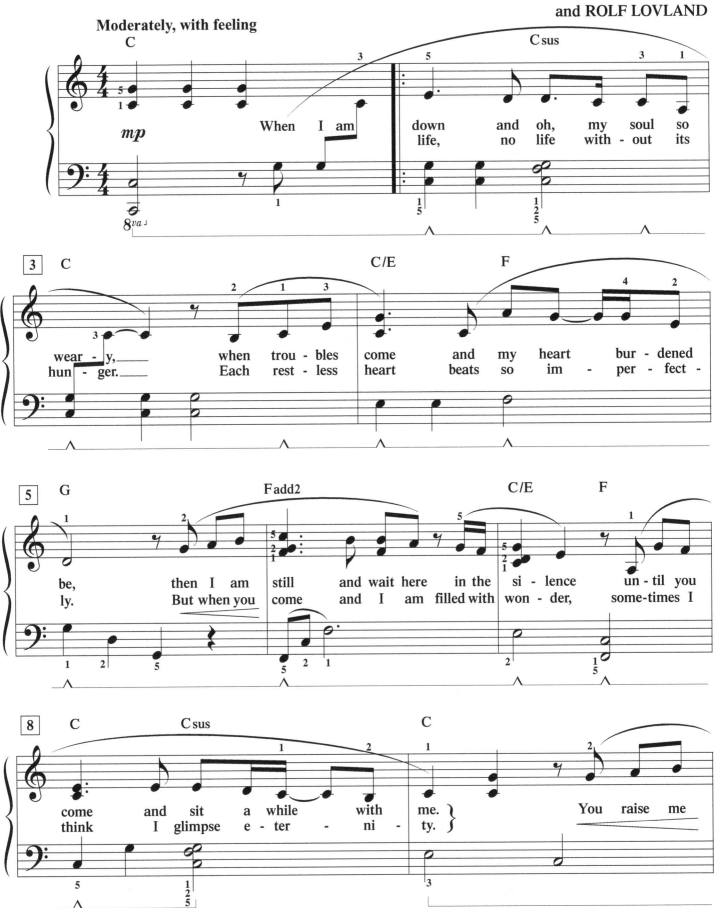

I Saw Her Standing There

Words and Music by
JOHN LENNON and PAUL MCCARTNEY

Fast dance beat

On Broadway

Words and Music by
BARRY MANN, CYNTHIA WEIL,
MIKE STOLLER, and JERRY LEIBER

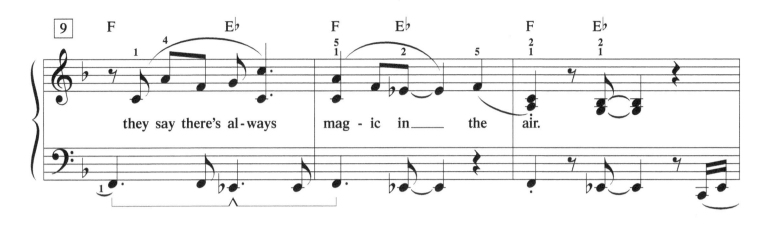

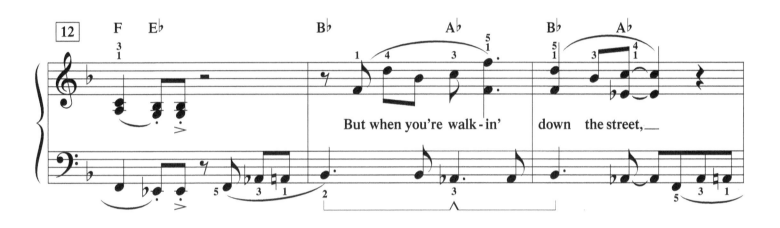

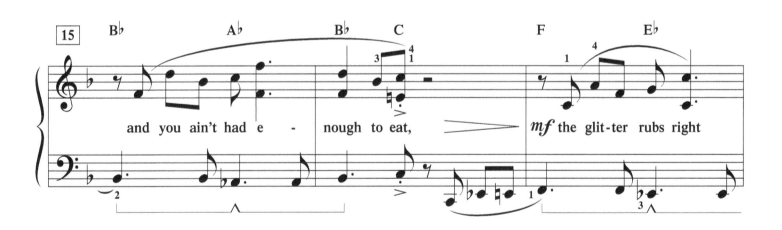

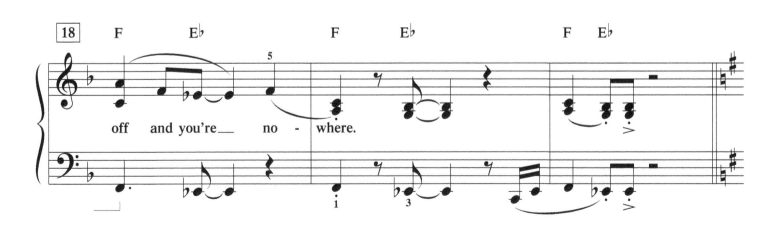

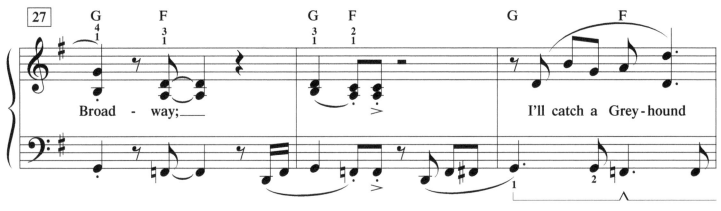

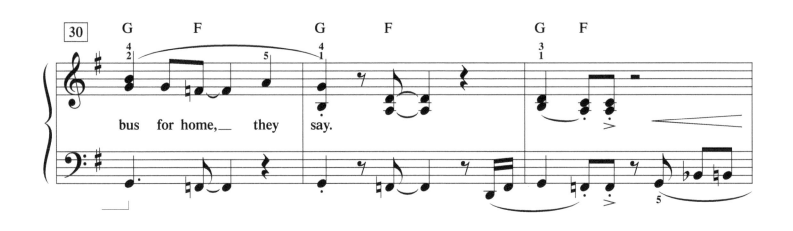

But they're dead wrong, I know they are, 'cause I can play this

here gui-tar. And I won't quit till I'm a star___ on

Broad - way.___ On Broad - way.___

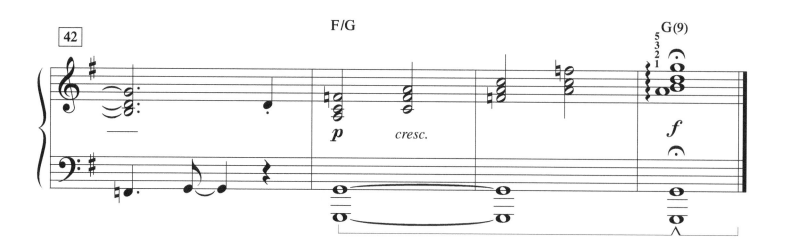

from Walt Disney Pictures' *Pirates of the Caribbean:*
The Curse of the Black Pearl

The Medallion Calls

Music by
KLAUS BADELT

35

FF1009

Pachelbel Canon

(Originally in the Key of D)

JOHANN PACHELBEL

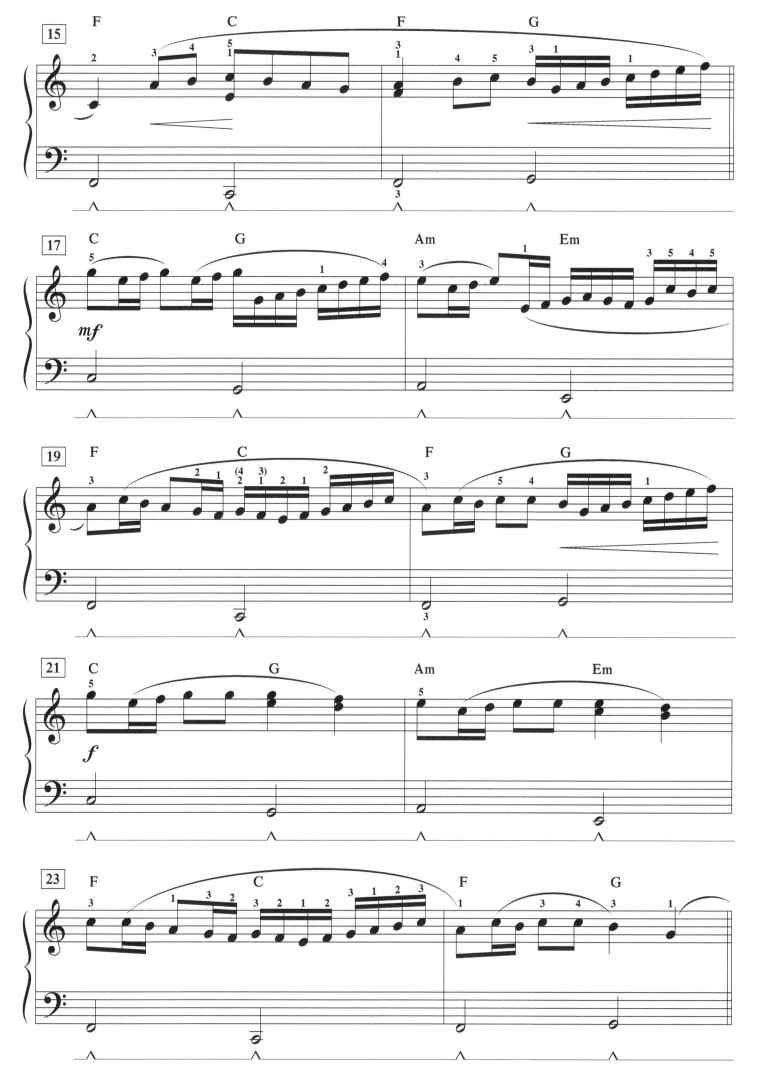